JAH ELLIOT

White-Collar Scholars

Fraud Masterminds

Contents

I

Get It How You Live

Life is a hustle. If you ain't producing you useless. In other words, you better off dead. As we all should know if you don't hustle you don't eat. It's that simple but the principle of hustling is often misconstrued. The entire purpose of hustling is to gain and get more. But not just more money the hustle brings you knowledge, structure, guidance, consistency, and most importantly a change to who you are. Everybody situation is different but no matter what you have to hustle.

1

Dedication

This literary piece is first and foremost dedicated to God for giving me the rhythm and ability to tell stories through writing. Secondly, this book is dedicated to those who enjoy reading perspective-driven literary pieces and stories of the unknown. Lastly, this story is dedicated to all individuals who hustle divinely.

2

Prologue

This story I am getting ready to tell is about two brothers who are identical twins, Kabi and Kahari. Like most black males, Kabi and Kahari were born and raised by a cursed family that eventually fell apart through the years. You know, a drug-addict mother, a father who was there but not present, a broken home, a God-fearing grandmother, and poverty are the setting and tone of everything around them. Although everything around them was the same, these brothers were different.

Different, as in they were outliers or out of place. Though their environment conveyed a different perspective, they saw it as an opportunity to impose a narrative that pharaohs still exist. Pharaohs do exist. Most are nameless, faceless, or too divine for people to see. To convey this story creatively and effectively, it needs to be told as if it were being said to you. This structure or form of writing in this book is termed *Jaheism,* a writing technique that I created to make reading more immersive and as if you were conversing with the book.

3

Times Is Hard

My earliest memory of life and consciousness was when I was like five. My mama was strung out on a bunch of shit, my dad was just institutionalized, and my granny was carrying the burdens of the dead and the living. I remember when we were at the corner store, and I wanted some candy. Like it was the jumbo, the pack of some gummies, it was like seven dollars. So, before I grabbed it, my granny say, "Kahari! Times is hard! I don't have it! Not for no candy, baby. Not right now."

At that time, I'm like four or five years old, but I understood what she was saying. I don't have enough money to buy any candy for seven dollars. It's not a need. So she ain't even gonna buy it because it's a waste. Which I know it would have been regardless. It was just some candy, and I knew that too. But what I didn't understand at the time was "times is hard." Because as a child you really not thinking about like money, struggling, bills, or anything relating to taking care of you and yours. But that's my earliest memory. Another thing that started to become apparent was time itself. Like shit changes but what was peculiar is the fact that when times change it's different from the past like generations of people, history, politics, the environment, the economy it's like everything of a particular time adapts for the future.

Even now times are completely different from before nothing is the same not even the sun and moon.

To a lot of muthafuckas that hear that they would say, "What you mean?"

What I mean by that is time changed so much people don't pay attention to what is now. For example, the sun could be somewhere in the sky and the moon could be somewhere but their position is bound to change through time. And as humans, we only pay attention to the sun and the moon when they are in a certain phase or position. Just like time in life. We only look a certain times based on the position we are in. That in itself was an epiphany. I was just lost and then God blessed me with that idea or point of view. My granny made sure me and Kabi was in that bible.

She used to say, "You wanna know who your real father is read the book of *Genesis*. The first book in the bible. Once you read that just keep on and you gonna see everything I tell y'all."

I kept those words with me. Always. I also keep my bible on me too. Because I was blessed with something I just can't explain. It's almost like I was blessed with knowledge and the glory of the lord. So, with all that being said as time went on me and brother saw everything my grandmother was saying. It's almost like she been through so much she understands the facets of life and what existence brings with it. Years go by and me and my brother just had our sixteenth birthday and our grandma was tired of dealing with our mama she was stealing money, wasn't paying the portion of her bills, out all night, getting all types of checks, and wasn't contributing my grandma got tired and all that worrying led her down to illness.

Illness meaning like she stop trying and couldn't take it anymore. On top of that what made her feel that way was me and my brother. She knew we saw everything from when we were toddlers to now. It was all just wickedness and it was too much for us all even my mama. It got to a point where my granny hated the thought of my mama. We did too. I just hate the fact it hurt her because it hurt us. But that was my granny's daughter. So she looked at it from a parent's perspective because she is a mother and a nurturer but it wasn't no nurturing my mama she lost from the jump.

Once my granny gave up she just didn't care about anything it's like for her times and things never change.

"So if it ain't gonna change, why try?

That was her mindset. Then a few weeks after she told us she was done as in with life she got sick. She had all types of shit but what hurt me and my bro was when the doctor said she had dementia. Me and bro cried. I never cried about nothing but that shit there killed a part of us. As I said before she had all types of shit but she had *Dementia* and *Lupus*. It was just crazy; better yet treacherous granny is all we ever had. Once she gone all I got is my bro. Once all that was put in the air we had to have a sit down because we had to get something going. When I say all I got is my bro that's all I have. My granny only had one child which is my mama, my granny's family broke apart when she was a lil girl and she was raised by her granny. It was just her and big mama the rest of her family was gone.

She always told us she wanted her child's life to be different but it was the exact same. Nothing ever changed and she felt like if she couldn't do it then nobody could. It happened all over again and she was just lost. She was tryna figure out how to make it stop or how to change it. She couldn't so she asked God to. But it all did change not for her or my mama but for us. Us as in me and my brother. Kabi. If you never know nothing else about Kabi that nigga is a gladiator and a hustler. I know that because I'm the same way with a different approach. After our granny explain everything to us we knew what time it was. It was time to get how we live. We needed to hustle. In our minds, we ain't care about what we had to do because granny needed her medicine and bills gon keep coming so me and Kabi just took some time to think. We would just be at home silent just thinking and checking on our granny.

The only conversation we had during them months after our granny was sick was a pact. We both agreed to keep our business between us, never change or lose ourselves, and be my brother's keeper. Then like I say Kabi is a… a… computer magician that nigga can make some money. Me I know I'm elegant with my words, concocting plans and communication which was perfect. That's all we needed everything else time was gon show. And it did.

4

Politicians

I ain't gon lie I was hurt matter of fact I was hurting. I was in so much pain but it was all mental. That shit crazy how something that is not even physical could hurt you. I always read books because my granny had me and Kahari in that bible. That bible educated a nigga so much to where I was like fuck it I'mma start reading. My granny had like a bookshelf full of books and I'll just pick one up and start reading. I read books about philosophy, education, romance, crime, satire, and urban books. Like reading for me was therapeutic because it helped my mind think about other shit and not what was going on around me or within the household.

My mama put us all through some shit we wasn't really ready for but it was meant for us to experience. Like I don't know how Kahari saw it but I felt like we didn't even matter. Our mama just ain't do shit for us and she was there but she wasn't present. Me and bro talked about that shit and came to our senses on that. Imagine seeing your mama every day and her not being a mom. She never cooked for us, bought us clothes, gave us no game, asked us how we was feeling, no affection, and never showed us no love man.

I tell you this right here. Man, it was our sixteenth birthday and my granny had asked us what we wanted and we told her some Jay's. It was some Retro four's coming out that weekend. We had a plug too so it was good all we needed was the bread. During that time we could just go to *Footlocker* wait in line and buy them hoes. The shoes was two hundred dollars a piece and my granny said my mama told her she was gon get us a gift. So we assume my granny told our mama we wanted the Jay's. Which she did. So our mama promised us dawg... she promised us she would get 'em. She told us over the phone. So, we thinking we finna get the Jay's. So our granny got us a matching outfit for our Jay's and that Saturday morning we was gon get 'em and be fly.

That Friday night we was waiting on our mama she always came home to sleep so we stayed up until midnight. She still ain't hit the door a couple of hours later. So, we was like fuck it she gon be here before the sun up. We went to sleep woke up and she wasn't there. It was seven in the morning. *Footlocker* open at eight so we was good. Seven forty-five came and she still wasn't there. My granny was in the hallway sitting in her chair gazing into the air.

I saw my granny face and thought to myself and said in my head, "we not getting them shoes."

Then Kahari looked at me with the same face. We knew. Another let down and broken promise all in one. We ain't even have no party or nothing we was gon get fly and go to movies and chill. But once nine-hit we just stayed at home all day. Our granny was pissed to the point she start crying. We told her don't worry about it we good so we just played the game and chilled. My granny was in her room she ain't even bother to call my mama or nothing. The next day came and my mama finally showed up and just didn't acknowledge our presence, birthday, or even say wassup. She had some food, a new purse, shoes, and nigga… she had the four's on. That was just at a glance though me, Kahari, and my granny solid-though we ain't even say nothing. But she was coming to get something she needed I guess. We hear a knock at the door and my bro opened the door. We see a nigga she fucking more than likely and he had the fours on too.

As my mama walked out the door my granny screamed, "Bitch is you crazy!? You must done lost yo damn mine hoe!?"

My mama turn around and just stood there for a moment. Then she said, "bitch who you talking to!?"

That nigga Kahari jumped up and got in my mama's face and said, "You! dick-sucking ass bitch!"

I was shook. I looked back down the hall at my granny she was shook too. For the first time, my mama came to her senses at that moment. She was looking at my brother like I don't even know.

Then my bro said, "Our birthday was yesterday bitch! Where was you!? Sucking dick or something!?"

My brother don't even raise his voice but that day he was fucked up. My mama was speechless. She was looking at my brother but she was talking to everybody. I was looking at her and I swear to God she said, "Kahari, Kabi, mama I'm sorry. I'm sorry. Look I'mma be back in a few. We can talk then. "

Tears started to come down her eyes she was fucked up about that. She just walked out of the house and tears fell down my bro eyes. I started crying and my granny like it was like a movie. I just laid down and that was it. That's all I remember. A few hours later our mama pulled back up, came in the house, and she had a box in her hands.

So she say, "Kahari!?"

Bro get up and walk to her. I get up out the bed and walk to the door and just started to pay attention. So my mama put the bag down and said, "I got you the Jay's you wanted."

Mind you she was drunk and high so she was outta there you could hear and see it. Plus she only had one pair of shoes. It was like fuck me. I was laughing in my head but she pulled the shoes out the box which was the four's. But they was laced differently from how they come in the box. The nigga that brought her to the house had the fours too. The same way he had them laced was the same way she pulled them out the box. I know my bro peeped that shit and I did too. The shoes had creases and shit and at the bottom, it looked like they had been worn before.

So my brother examined the shoe and he say, "These the Jay's that nigga had on? You bought these for another nigga and yourself and not you kids? Then you try to give them to me cuz we wear the same size?"

My mama broke down boy. She cried hard and my brother had no emotions or gave in to her crying. I knew bro was solid because that shit was not real. It didn't feel real either. My granny finally walked up to the front door grabbed my brother and walked him into her room. So I followed them my granny just hugged my brother and I was standing there.

We was just in there thinking and you can hear our mama in there crying. She started to scream, "I'm fucked up y'all! My baby daddy lied to me, my dreams got shattered, I got on that dope, people turning they back on me, I started fuck around doing other shit and ain't been the same since! Mama, I know you tried but I just can't!"

That shit hurt my granny. Why? I don't know maybe

because that's her daughter but to us, that was an excuse. Just because something happen to you don't mean you take it out on everybody else. Basically, what I'm saying is that if you suffering don't make people suffer because you are.

My grandmother always said, "Misery needs company."

Boy, she wasn't lying. My mama just left and she left the shoes but after our granny explained everything thoroughly to us. We knew where my granny's head was she basically explained how she felt as a mom to a pathetic daughter. That was just one situation. I'm not even finna go into detail on other shit it's too much to even think about. But me and bro made a vow we gon make sure that our kids don't go through that and we stay with some money. The next day my mama came back and gave us three hundred dollars a piece the first and last thing she did for us that meant something to us. She talked to my granny and didn't come back until we had our hustle going. I'll get to that.

Me and bro sat on that three-hundred we wanted to see how we can flip it. As we was discussing that our granny told us to call nine-one-one she was feeling bad. We get to the doctor and he had a list of shit wrong with her. We took that heart and needed to show some too. They diagnosed her and the doctor was explaining all the shit.

Kahari was listening more than me and the doctor say, "She may be on the verge of death. So what do you guys have planned for her?" I told that nigga, "To hustle and make sure she straight."

The white boy understood and he basically said he was willing to work with us. So we told him to stay in contact with us. They got her right and we skated home. She was straight but she needed somebody to check on her from time to time. Her illnesses and diseases wasn't severe she just had a lot going on with herself.

he even got to the door I was looking out the window and seen 'em. I opened the door and that nigga handed me and Kahari six hundred a piece. We chopped it up and we both gave him three hundred out of our six. We ain't ask no questions he says he gon be coming back with more. We knew he was good for it. Black was lil older than us but he was cool with our granny because he work at the corner store around the corner. So we was good plus he had two daughters so he gotta get it.

As far as the website Kahari printed out flyers and we took our granny *Pontiac* drove downtown and put flyers all through there for the website. Once we hit downtown we hit rich neighborhoods, retail stores, and schools in those areas. That shit took like four of five hours. Once we posted that last one up we headed home. Got home chilled with granny and just waited. We knew something was finna happen so we just let time speak.

Kahari's homegirl hit him like a week or so after and said, "Finna drop off all these envelopes to you."

I remember because he told me to look out for the house phone. She pulled up and handed Kahari a wad envelopes some of them hoes was thick too. My granny come out of the room to see if it was her ratchet-ass daughter. She saw it was for Kahari and went back into the room. His homegirl ain't ask no questions either so we was good. From what he told me, he told her it was for our family member's attorneys, paperwork from jail, and for money for his kids for the upcoming school year. She bought that shit too. She ain't open nothing, put everything nice and neat in a brown bag, and put a rubber band on the envelopes.

Once they get done we walk into the room and laid all the envelopes across the bed it was ninety-two of them hoes.

16

We opened up the thickest one and that hoe had twenty-five hundred dollars cash. Every envelope we opened we went half on that hoe. If it had five dollars in the envelope we each get two dollars and fifty cents. Simple as I told him. After we got done we had made ten-thousands dollars. Five bands each. I was looking at the bread like what the fuck. All these politicians in my hand and it's fuck the law. We was happy. We knew it was wrong but we gotta get it how we live.

After a while, I asked him, "Let me see the website." I was curious to see because them white folk giving out free money. When I saw the website that hoe looked like a Fortune five-hundred company website. That nigga Kahari put a nice logo, mission statement, who we are, why we are passionate about education, statistics on kids in need, why donating to educational organizations is important, fake employees, and a bunch of other shit.

But what set it off that nigga put, "We want all donators to remain anonymous and spread our organization through word of mouth. Any and every donation is appreciated."

I was like damn. We good. Now, all we needed to do was set up a few plays to get more money, and if anything go wrong we was straight. But that wasn't even important but what was important was the political aspect of the money we had coming. Basically, we wanted people to feel like their contributions, efforts, and trust was in the right hands. All in all, it was in the right hands. I praise the lord and put up both hands. Ya feel me.

5

Maneuver

Life wild. Life wild as hell. We made ten racks in a week and didn't even have to move. Me and Kabi counted that shit a million times. That was our first time ever making money together, our first hustle, and start to the *"American Dream."* A few days later Black came to the house and gave us nine hundred a piece. The first time we ain't bother to ask questions but this time we needed to talk business. I wanted everybody to be clear of they position, plays, and money. But before that, I wanted to lay some morals and ethics.

So, I told Black and Kabi come to the car and let's chop it up. They came to the car and they was ready. When I seen just they posture, demeanor, and body language I knew it wasn't gon take long.

Kabi say, "Let us know something." So I did.

First thing was to set standards of our partnership and understand how Black was making his money. As far as ethics, morals, and principles I said, "First we all in this for the money. We don't win if we fucking over the money, or shorting each other. Next, the main rules of this is to not bring you potnas in, tell you potnas, tell a female, lie about a situation, and last get greedy."

Black and Kabi both shook my hand. It was understood matter fact overstood. Before I even asked Black about how he was making his money he told us right then and there. I wasn't asking because I was scared he was gone get caught, or because he may play us, I was asking to know how to calculate the money when we invested some to him. Reason why we can know how to maneuver the money we was getting from the website. So, Black finally start talking about how we was making money and how he was breaking it down with us.

"Aight look. Y'all boys let me know if y'all understand this shit. If I lose you say something."

Me and Kabi shook our heads in agreeance and he spilled it to us.

"Y'all niggas know I work at the corner store. It is all type of bitches and niggas coming through there. I met a bitch. A white bitch that sell pussy. She don't look like a prostitute at all but she is. Well, she told me she was an escort. She just moved out here and needed to make bread."

Now mind you this nigga told us this but I was confused already. Kabi was too. I saw it in his eyes. I told these niggas, "Don't tell a bitch." I was thinking he told her but I let him speak.

Then Black say, "I asked her what you do and shit? She say, "I sell pussy." I'm shid cool."

We laugh hard as fuck because niggas pitiful and hungry at the same time.

"Nah real shit. Everybody who know me or know of my name Black don't bullshit a bullshitter. Ya feel me. So she tell that she need a car and people who interested. This was the same day y'all talk to me about what y'all wanted to do. I took the six from that I had made some fake photos, of all the "goods" bought with the money to make it seem like it was a real donation and that *Supplythechildren dot com* could be a trusted organization. I also made an email list, and keep track of phone numbers because I recommend that on flyers and websites for people who donate. Of those who donated I sent out emails of the flyers, updates, and money raised to make everything legit.

With all that being in motion I also put contact information for all inquiries and questions but the number was a pre-paid cell phone, and the email was just a burner email. Last what I did before I even made the website I used generic white people names, prestigious biographies, and direct emails which were all fake. But, I responded to emails and checked them every day. By doing that it makes us look legitimate and transparent. We also passed out flyers but on the flyers I put, "Flyer brought to you by our journeyman."

When I told Kabi that he say, "You tryna get us caught up huh!?" I said, "Nah, bro I did that to make it seem like they paid us to work with them as people who carry out messages for the organization. That way if we get caught in something we can say we met a white man downtown once he paid us cash to put out flyers but, we never saw him ever again."

"So what about the P.O. Box?" If that's your homegirl's shìt and somehow all this caught up to us how we gon maneuver?" Kabi asked a good question but the answer is the same. "He paid her to use her P.O. box. As in *Billy Bocha* the CEO of *Supplythechildren dot com*."

Kabi shook his head. It was the perfect plan but we still had money to make and ten thousand dollars plus cash on us. It wasn't a lot of money we understood that but we couldn't just go crazy with it or bring people in. It was May and school was basically three months away. So we had time to get it and be straight. The only issue now was our granny she ain't play that shit. So we had to have a solid cover for the money we was making. The only way was to get a nine to five. She would think we getting work money. Me and Kabi agreed but it was one last issue. The one issue that concerned me the most... if the people donating find out the organization is fraud which it is how we gon get out of that shit? I asked myself that shit so many times but it wasn't nothing to be concerned about at the moment. Why? Because we moving like we are legit. But like I said we had time. I could just come up with some shit in the meantime. Once August hit set up fake charity events, pictures of kids taking photos with backpacks and school supplies, and keep going the same shit.

"Kahari so we really gon go out and buy all that shit foreal?" Kabi ask me that dumbass shit and didn't look at him. I just answered. I say, "Kabi all we gotta do is buy a few things. Once we do that find a group of kids take a pictures of them with the shit, take the supplies back, and give them a few dollars. Easy." If you offer a child money they gon take it plus we gon get the cheapest shit we can find. Pens, pencils, paper, and all that cheap. Bulk up on it and just take photos and upload them on the site. As long as we maneuver correctly everything else will be fine. Best way to move is silent because nothing can be mistaken when the money is talking. Real nigga shit.

6

Square Business

Kahari really set the tone. I know I put it out there but bro set a standard. Street niggas ain't eating like us. It's only like three of four weeks since we started all that shit. But Kahari was in that mode that *flow state*. Where you just moving and improving. Every day he explaining new shit with the website. The shit was so interesting because he had a passion for computers and being able to make money off it glued him to it.

Everyday, "Kabi come here real quick." I used to sit there and pay attention to everything. But it wasn't because of the money but the hustle he put into to get it. The foundation, the structure, the organization, the strategy, and all that stood out to me more. It was also shown through the website. This nigga Kahari like he told me had the site broke up five different pieces. Food, clothing, supplies, extracurricular activities, and he had one he kept changing and just putting additional needs. But he had it to where each of the five categories had their limit and restrictions. Meaning he set a monthly amount of donations and money that should be contributed. Each category had a maximum donation of three-thousand dollars a month. Once the goal was reached for that category you couldn't donate anymore. But the thing is you still could we taking cash.

Then when people sent donations on the site he said, "Write down where you want your money to go."

All of that was to make the site seem legit, on our end make it easy to manage and keep track of the money. Even if we didn't make the total fifteen we still could manage that money properly and easily. But I was looking at it long-term. If it is five categories three-thousand times five is fifteen thousand. If you put that in a year that's damn there two-hundred thousand dollars.

After he explained all that shit and I understood I got hit with a idea that was gone change everything. If I learn to do this shit I can make websites on my own and say we are partners with *Supplythechildren dot com.* That way if we do it right people can't pinpoint who is who or track the money once, or if something goes wrong we can easily get off it. Simple. I knew it was a lot more to it but time was gon show all that. Then we had the hustle with Black. Queen wasn't bringing us no money, money. Like if she charging niggas four-hundred to fuck and she only fuck one nigga that's a hunnit dollars. Which it got slow because that's too much for pussy being delivered to you.

Kahari wasn't really too much worried about it because the site was the main hustle. But I thought to myself and had the best way to solve that issue. Give black money to re-up on drugs. But I thought to myself and was like that is too much of a risk. I really ain't know shit about drugs, prices, and I ain't trust niggas so fuck that. But what I did know the doctor that diagnose my was granny was off for a white boy. Off as in, he felt like a nigga.

Before we left the hospital I said, "We gin hit you." He said,

25

7

Faceless

After seeing Black and Queen exchanging that money, hearing how Kahari felt, and where this shit could go at any given moment, it ain't no telling what could happen. Black was doing his thang and handing us chump change, but it ain't no telling what else he is doing. Then he pimping with a white bitch. Another thing I noticed while we was sliding that Kahari had a blank face. He was thinking the same thing I was.

Black told us all the dope money was his money. But he already got Queen a truck, she fucking niggas, and how this setup we getting paid by Queen technically. But we had gave Black three hundred dollars out of six hundred he brought us the first time and back-doored and gave us nine. What he told us sounded good, but it was something in between that. I ain't know what, but I know Kahari had a plan. On real shit, I started to think harder because I felt that Black was cheating us. Once he again he ain't cheating us he cheating our granny.

Out of nowhere, Kahari says, "I might have to leave this nigga faceless. Something ain't making sense. Just remain my brother, all the way through Kabi."

www.ingramcontent.com/pod-product-compliance
Lightning Source LLC
LaVergne TN
LVHW051752050326
832903LV00029B/2871